# Explaining
# Hearing from
# God

## Peter H. Lawrence

**Sovereign World**

God bless, Love, sis

All Scripture quotations are from
the NIV The Holy Bible, New International Version.
© Copyright 1973, 1978 International Bible Society.
Published by Hodder & Stoughton.

ISBN: 1 85240 086 2

SOVEREIGN WORLD LIMITED
P.O. Box 777, Tonbridge, Kent TN11 9XT, England.

# *Contents*

# Contents

# 1

# Is There a Word
# from the Lord?

The phone rang in my study. It was Harold. He had recently moved from his position as pastor of our local full-gospel church in Birmingham to take up a similar vocation in Whitley Bay. This was a welcome call from an old friend.

"Hello Peter," he began, and after exchanging a few pleasantries came to the point. "How do you feel about coming and doing an evening meeting for us just after Easter?" he asked.

"Delighted Harold," I replied without thinking about it.

As I put the phone down I began to have second thoughts. I reached for an atlas. I had no idea where Whitley Bay was situated. I eventually found it on the other side of Newcastle-upon-Tyne; it was a round trip of about 400 miles.

Once I had recovered from the initial shock and prayed much for my ageing car, the journey was not too bad. Three others came with me as we visited friends in Leeds, called in to see Durham Cathedral and stood beneath a collection of impressive bridges at the Tyneside docks. Harold's house overlooked the crashing waves of the North Sea. This was not quite the same as land-locked industrial Birmingham. and yet... I could not relax and enjoy any of it.

I'd spent a little time in prayer before leaving Birmingham, talking things through with God and waiting expectantly in the silences for God to speak to me. One simple thought had come into my head: "There will be a lady at the meeting with one weak leg due to poliomyelitis as a child. She does not walk too well as a result of this."

Such thoughts are always very worrying. How do we know when it is God speaking? I discussed it with the other end of the dialogue in my mind. "What do you want me to do? How shall I give the word? Is that it or are there any more?" I asked, taking a chance it was God communicating with me. "Give it in the middle of your sermon," God seemed to say, "as an example of the importance of risk-taking. If the lady is there and claims the 'word' say this to her: 'I believe God is wanting to encourage you to lay hands on the sick and pray for them. Do not let your own disability stop you from doing so as it has given you a greater sensitivity to those who are ill.' " There were no other 'words'.

The stillness of the moment was followed by an awesome silence. No further thoughts. One 'word' for one person received a day before the meeting. At other meetings I had always shared several 'words' and asked people to come forward together. Some were nearly always claimed and the possible embarrassment was over. This time there was only one thought – maybe mine – maybe from God – maybe a deception – how can anyone know?

For twenty-four hours I was alone with my thoughts. The rest of the world seemed to be going on without me, somewhere out there. Inside I was dominated by another world of insecurity and fear. "What if…?" I'd heard these words from Satan before. "If I'm wrong," I replied, "I receive all the blame. If I'm right God gets all the glory." It was enough to keep him at bay for a while.

During the long journey he came again. "What if the church is full of extremists who don't believe Christians should ever be ill, and lame ones should certainly never minister to others?" "Then," I replied, "they really do need to hear this 'word'." Faith, hope and love are the characteristics of God's kingdom. Condemnation belongs to the other one. I knew if this 'word' was correct it would take away condemnation, increase faith, provide hope and encourage love. In a strange way Satan's attacks strengthened my belief and resolve.

Obedience to what I thought God was saying lay before me as the only way to overcome fear. We pressed on to our destination.

Harold said the meeting would start at half past seven; he would lead worship until about eight o'clock, and then I'd be on. It was nearer to nine than eight when I stood up; I had been to pentecostal meetings before and I did know Harold; but it still did not make waiting any easier.

As I made the point about the importance of risk-taking in seeing God's signs and wonders, I slipped in my 'word' as an example. "Is there a lady here who suffered from polio as a child and now has one weak leg?" I asked. Twenty-four hours of anxiety and pain was over in a flash. There was a brief pause and then a brave lady stood up. As she did so the calliper on her left leg became visible to me for the first time. She confirmed the 'word' fitted her exactly. "I think God may be saying," I continued tentatively, "that he wants you to feel free to lay hands on the sick and pray for them. I believe your own disability which has held you back in the past has in fact given you greater sensitivity to the needs of others. I think God now wants to release you into this ministry."

There seemed to be a little hum of confirmation and approval from those present who knew the lady well. I asked her if she felt she could accept the 'word' and she nodded before sitting down.

Shortly afterwards I asked God the Father through Jesus to send his Holy Spirit upon us. By then there was already a corporate sense that 'God was in this place'. It was no surprise to see the vast majority registering openness to God on their faces; beaming countenances showing God's love and peace; and some physical signs of shaking and falling which indicated the presence of God's power. The 'word' seemed to have prepared the people for his coming among them. Many felt very blessed by God.

In this brief account of my visit to Whitley Bay we can identify five different activities which enabled the 'word from God' to accomplish its purpose:-

1. God spoke

2. The word was recognised

3. The word was given

4. The word was claimed

5. The word was confirmed.

In learning to hear from God I consider all of these five areas to be important. I shall look at each in turn.

# 2

# The God Who
# Speaks

Christianity is a revealed religion. Christians believe God has revealed himself to us throughout history and most especially in his son Jesus Christ. We do not make up or think through what it would be good to believe about God or choose a god we would like to serve. Our aim is not to make God in our own image. We believe what God has shown of himself to us, and seek to obey his word. This means our God is a God who speaks. He has taken the initiative and communicated with us. He is not a dumb idol.

The Bible testifies from beginning to end that our God is a God who speaks. He speaks in words and visions and prophecies; he speaks in history; he speaks through his son Jesus Christ; he speaks through the early Church as the Holy Spirit is poured out upon all believers. He is a God who calls his children into a personal and living relationship with himself. He is a communicating God.

The history of the Christian Church confirms the testimony of Scripture.

According to Eusebius and Lactanius in 312 A.D. Constantine saw a vision and later received instructions in a dream prior to his battle with Maxentius for the city of Rome. He was instructed to put the sign of the Christian cross on his soldiers' equipment and against most expectations was victorious. Constantine went on to become the Roman Emperor and ended the official persecutions of Christians.

Following conversations with his Christian friend Alipius the

9

worldly Augustine went into the garden and began to weep with repentance for his many sins. As he did so he heard a sweet voice which he thought to be a girl singing nearby and then the words, 'Take up and read.' He returned to the house, opened the epistles of Paul and read the first passage he saw. *'Let us behave decently, as in the daytime, not in sexual immorality and debauchery, not in dissension and jealousy. Rather, clothe yourselves with the Lord Jesus Christ, and do not think about how to gratify the desires of the sinful nature'* (Romans 13:13, 14). He was so moved he was converted to Christianity and became one of its most famous saints.

The history of Christianity is full of stories of both famous and unknown people who testify to hearing and knowing the God who speaks. These people have received individual words of guidance which complemented the general and doctrinal words of Scripture.

There have also been many inspired writings and other kinds of communications from God since the days of the early Church and the writing of the Bible. Scripture and history confirm the God who speaks, and support one another. Even so, the Christian Church has always maintained since the canon of Scripture was closed that the Bible has unique canonical authority. This is not because God has stopped speaking but because those who knew God uniquely as he revealed himself in the earthly Lord Jesus have all died.

Peter writes, *'We did not follow cleverly invented stories when we told you about the power and coming of our Lord Jesus Christ, but we were eye-witnesses of his majesty.'*     (2 Peter 1:16)

John wrote, *'That which was from the beginning, which we have heard, which we have seen with our eyes, which we have looked at and our hands have touched – this we proclaim concerning the Word of life.'*     (1 John 1:1)

These people knew the earthly Lord Jesus intimately. When the Spirit of Jesus subsequently revealed things to them and the early

Church they were able to test one against the other. Peter gave scriptural status to Paul's writings (2 Peter 3: 15, 16). We no longer have people who knew the earthly Jesus and listened to his teachings, so we cannot be as certain when God speaks today. The early Church tested their 'words' against their intimate knowledge of Jesus. We test ours against the early Church's words as found in the New Testament. God has spoken in the Bible and God does speak today. He is the God who speaks. The Bible has greater authority especially doctrinally because it was verified by those who knew Jesus.

The Bible and history bear witness not only to the God who speaks, but that the God who speaks lives in every believer. The writer to the Hebrews writes about the New Covenant between God and his people, made possible through the blood of Jesus (Hebrews 9:14, 15). He quotes Jeremiah:

*This is the covenant I will make with the house of Israel after that time, declares the Lord. I will put my laws in their minds and write them on their hearts. I will be their God, and they will be my people. No longer will a man teach his neighbour, or a man his brother, saying, 'Know the Lord,' because they will all know me, from the least of them to the greatest.*

(Hebrews 8: 10, 11)

Those who choose to enter the New Covenant through the blood of Jesus will know the Lord, *'from the least of them to the greatest'*. Isaiah suggests this promise is everlasting:

*"The Redeemer will come to Zion, to those in Jacob who repent of their sins." declares the Lord. "As for me, this is my covenant with them," says the Lord. "My Spirit, who is on you, and my words that I have put in your mouth will not depart from your mouth, or from the mouths of your children, or from the mouths of their descendants from this time on and for ever," says the Lord.* (Isaiah 59:20, 21)

How is this possible?

11

> *'God has poured out his love into our hearts by the Holy Spirit, whom he has given us.'* (Romans 5:5)

Once we have received the Holy Spirit he lives in us.

> *'Don't you know that you yourselves are God's temple and that God's Spirit lives in you?'* (1 Corinthians 3:16)

This distinguishes Christians from non-Christians.

> *'And if anyone does not have the Spirit of Christ, he does not belong to Christ.'* (Romans 8:9)

How do we become a Christian and receive the Holy Spirit? In Acts 2 after Peter has preached the crucified, risen, ascended Christ as the one who baptises in the Holy Spirit, the people believe and ask what to do. Peter says:

> *'Repent and be baptised, every one of you, in the name of Jesus Christ for the forgiveness of your sins. And you will receive the gift of the Holy Spirit. The promise is for you and your children and for all who are far off – for all whom the Lord our God will call.'* (Acts 2:38, 39)

So, whoever wants to become a Christian needs to:

(a) Believe and trust in Jesus
(b) Repent of their sins
(c) Be baptised
(d) Receive the Holy Spirit

Once we have done this the God who speaks lives inside us by his Holy Spirit. When this happens the prophecy of Jeremiah begins to be fulfilled in us. *'We have the mind of Christ'* (1 Corinthians 2:16).

This, then, is the truth of Scripture. Our God is the God who speaks, who loves to be known by his children and to communicate with them. Everyone who is born again by water and Spirit has the God who speaks living inside them. The obvious conclusion is that every Christian should expect to hear God speaking to them directly from time to time.

The difference in my own life once I realised the God who speaks lives inside me was quite profound. While being careful not to afford canonical or doctrinal status to any revelation I believed came from God, I nevertheless began to look for and to expect day to day promptings, nudgings and guidance.

One weekend in 1991, church attendance was greatly affected by deep snow. All but the major roads were blocked and everyone was advised to stay indoors except for emergencies. I looked forward to a pleasant and relaxing Monday. My children could not get to school; no-one would expect me to visit them; I could stay late in bed and spend the day pottering about.

It was not to be. I awoke at eight o'clock with a sense of urgency all over me. I prayed while still in bed, "Lord, why do I feel like this?" The answering thought in my mind was instant: "Get up immediately. I want you to go and visit Rose in hospital right now." This was an unwelcome idea and very impractical. My garage is built on a steep, narrow incline. My car had not been out for days. My garage door and drive were blocked with four or five feet of snow and the hospital was several miles away.

I reminded God of these facts. Silly, really, but I did my best to argue the case for staying in bed. I lost. The sense of urgency persisted so I arose, dressed, grabbed a cup of coffee and a shovel and made for the garage to the incredulous surprise of my wife, Carol.

"Hospital visit," I offered apologetically with a shrug of the shoulders. "God told me." Carol smiled and kissed me on my way. I took giant steps in my wellies, making deep holes in the snow as I went. The fierce wind had swept large drifts against the garage door and as I began to dig for God, several local teenagers gathered to jeer me on. The car was surprised to see me and reluctant to leap about but eventually, after considerable revving, we rushed backwards down the slope, sliding narrowly past the wall and nearby tree. "Maybe it was God speaking after all," I thought as the car and I made it safely to the hospital.

I was at Rose's bedside by half past nine. The curtains were drawn around her bed as she was unconscious and struggling for breath. Having arrived, I now didn't know what to do. Rose was eighty-four and had been a faithful member of our church for some time. "Pray in tongues," was the suggestion which formed in my mind. I did this for a few minutes then, as I drew to a close, the thought came, "Keep going." As I obeyed, light seemed to come into the area, and power and heat came on my body. "Now," a new thought interrupted me, "now you can lay hands on Rose." I did so gently. Distress on her face seemed to give way to peace. Power flowed through my hands. I prayed my best prayers and committed Rose into the hands of God. After this I stood back and stayed put for another five minutes. There seemed to be a powerful yet peaceful spiritual presence. I didn't really want to leave. Rose, though unconscious, seemed to be all right. "You've finished now," came the thought. "You can go." Reluctantly I turned and made my way slowly back to the car. Amazingly I made it home, up the slope and into the garage totally unscathed.

Later Rose's daughter rang me. When they had arrived at ten o'clock the same morning, her mother was dead. As she told me it was difficult not to say I already knew. For some reason God wanted me to be present and pray before Rose died. Maybe in some way it eased her passing, but whatever the reason I felt sure my sense of urgency and the message I received came from God.

**Summary**

* The God and Father of our Lord Jesus Christ is the God who speaks.

✻ The God who speaks lives inside every born-again believer, by his Spirit.

✻ As the God who speaks lives inside every believer, it seems reasonable to suggest that all Christians should expect to receive direct God-given messages from time to time.

# 3

# Recognising
# God's Voice

The first major breakthrough for me in hearing God speak was when I grasped the biblical truth that the God who speaks lives in me. The second was the testimony of others. What I had so often classed as 'premonitions', 'coincidences' or 'uncanny feelings' I now realised had probably been God all the time.

In Britain we live in a very cynical society. Even in church circles the suggestion, "I think God may have said to me ..." has often been met in the past with the derisory comment, "Got a hot line to God, have we?" Such negative remarks caused me to relegate 'hearing God' to the odd and gifted few and I would have required an angel writing on the wall, or a blinding flash to persuade me I was among them.

I am now totally convinced every born again Christian does have the Spirit of God within them, giving a direct hot line to God. The problem is that most Christians do not know this and do not recognise the call when it comes. I was amazed when I first heard people say things like, "I received a pain in my knee as I prayed, and knew someone present had a knee problem," or, "I saw a picture in my mind of a left leg broken in two places," or, "the word 'neuralgia' came into my mind." Simple communications using our natural senses which when given in small meetings led to ministry, healing or blessing and often advanced God's kingdom.

Because the Spirit of the God who speaks is in all Christians we who are born again can all be receivers of God's messages. Invariably his 'words' will then be a part of us, registered in our bodies, feelings and minds. The difficulty in teaching others how to recognise God's voice is that every receiver is different. In effect every person is unique and we all need to learn for ourselves how our own receiver works.

Several times I have been in meetings when Bill Subritzky has smelt the fragrance of God's presence. He often recognises God's anointing in this way – when to lay on hands and minister and when to hold back. He always refuses to minister unless he senses God's anointing. Sometimes he asks others, "Can you smell God's fragrance?" and people nod or raise their hands. I have never smelt anything.

John Wimber sometimes sees words flashing across his mind like ticker-tape and has seen words on balconies, people's foreheads or in the sky. The only times I see words on people's faces is when my daughters have been playing with felt tip pens.

I have known one person register fear, another anger and a third go very cold when they have discerned demons in a person. On the other hand, I regularly find my hands heat up when I sense God wants me to minister to someone and occasionally my heart has thumped wildly when a prophetic message has formed in me at a meeting.

I am sure it is the same Holy Spirit at work within us and yet because we are all different the manifestations vary enormously according to personality, home background, culture, individuality and gifting. In hearing God, who is within us, I think it is important we try to discover how our own receiver works, and this invariably means trial and error.

In order to evaluate what may be from God and what is definitely not, I believe we need to begin asking God for messages which are either provably right or provably wrong. To stand up in a gathering of several hundred and say, "I believe God is saying there is someone here with back trouble," will never tell us whether we are hearing God or not. Similarly, to expect a congregation to accept a long prophecy as from God when the person giving it has never been known to be right before, is unreasonable. We need to risk being wrong so that we can also learn when we are right.

Each day I try to find some time to be alone with God, preferably in the morning. Then as well as worshipping, reading the Bible and praying, I normally ask my heavenly Father through Jesus to send his Holy Spirit upon me. Sometimes in the silence I may feel power or heat; often I find thoughts come to me about the day or those for whom I have prayed. "Visit this person first, then the others." I did that the other day and found a lady and her husband about to go out. "I'm so pleased you've just caught us," she said. "Five minutes later and we'd have been out all afternoon."

Last week, I was in a meeting and during some prayers the idea came to me. "Go and visit Jim. Leave the meeting after the talk but before the end and visit Jim." I waited until the talk was over, slipped out during the coffee break and found Jim had been in just a few minutes when I arrived. Jim's wife Sue had died suddenly at the age of 35 leaving him with three children. It was good to squeeze in a time to chat in our busy lives. He also gave me a splendid lunch. Apparently the ending of the meeting I missed would not have been particularly relevant for me.

Such simple guidance is very undramatic, not at all convincing for the sceptic, but totally unthreatening for the beginner. Asking God to give simple 'words' that can be found to be provably right or provably wrong without hurting anyone is a good place to start. A few locked doors with nobody in suggests we may need to wait longer in prayer, but to keep trying. It is certainly not yet the time to be standing up in meetings declaring, "God says …".

From such simple beginnings and being willing to risk all non-threatening messages at the start, I have been able to discover quite a bit about my own receiver.

Nearly every time I have been woken in the night with a 'word' or a vivid dream, it has not been from God. Information contained in the message has invariably been found to be wrong. Other friends I have find dreams and middle-of-the-night communications to be far more accurate than at most other times and almost need to go to sleep to hear God.

There are times on my own when physical sensations have acted like the ringing of the telephone. A wave of heat across the forehead, a sudden surge of power, a change in breathing rhythm or heart beat have alerted me to the fact that God wants to communicate. When this happens the message is often very accurate. More frequently this does not occur and then the weeks, months and years of trial and error – seeking to discover how my own receiver works best – is my main source of learning to recognise God's voice.

If I am feeling at peace with God following a time of confession, repentance, worship and Bible-reading then I normally take seriously any specific thoughts which come to me. If they are in keeping with God's character as revealed in the Bible, I usually act upon them. If I receive difficult or odd 'words' which do not contradict Scripture I frequently ask for a confirming sign before assuming they may be from God.

At calm moments when I ask God to fill me afresh with his Holy Spirit I also take note of any sharp pains in my body which are not normal for me; any sudden feelings such as depression, sadness, guilt or despair; and any pictures or images which form in my mind. Sometimes when I have written them down the pain, feeling or visual communication will then disappear, only to come back again at the right moment or situation during the day when God wants me to act upon what I have received.

I remember before one small healing meeting sensing several individual sharp pains in different parts of my body, one after the other. I described them all at the service and found each one corresponded to a person present with a complaint in that area.

20

Prior to speaking at another small fellowship a feeling of sadness and pain came all over me. During my sermon it came again so I paused and spoke out words which came into my head about difficult and painful times ahead for the church. They were not particularly keen on the message when I gave it but when it was subsequently fulfilled it helped them to keep going without disbanding, until God brought them through into blessings.

On one occasion I saw in my mind a lady dressed in a particular way with very distinctive earrings. I was quite amazed to see this lady exactly as I had pictured her, giving the books out at the back of the church where I went to speak that night. God's Spirit came powerfully as we laid hands on her after the meeting.

Initially, I was not very good at being spontaneous, needing to receive any 'words' God wanted to give me some time before a meeting. This was the way it happened before going to Whitley Bay.

On the other hand my friend John Leach, a clergyman in the Coventry Diocese, tended to be a far more spontaneous personality than myself and from the start often heard from God in the situation. This meant I expected to hear before meetings or encounters, looking for some details during my morning prayer time while John expected to hear during a meeting or encounter and treated his quiet-time a little differently.

After several years of writing messages down the day before meetings or expecting God's daily guidance during my early morning prayers, things gradually began to change. I had always thought I could not be spontaneous like John but the expectant prayerful Body of Christ has helped me a great deal.

In group prayer times when others are interceding powerfully, my own receiver often now gets a clearer message than when on my own. I remember praying for Birmingham with others when I saw a vision of angels; the more others prayed and worshipped, the more distinct became the picture and message. I also began to find when I was ministering in a church service, particularly where the congregation was a believing, praying, worshipping one, 'words' on the spot started coming into my mind, frequently proving to be quite accurate.

As a result, there has now been a transition from always needing to receive before a gathering to almost becoming the spokesperson of the faithful assembly. Sometimes people have prayed for me to receive 'words' which I have then done. On one occasion Stuart arrived at one of our meetings suffering from hay fever. He prayed silently, "O Lord, if you want me to have prayer for this please give Peter a 'word' tonight." As we came to a time of ministry in the smallish group I said, "Could anyone suffering from hay fever please stand up." Stuart received prayer and felt much better. Gifts are given for the upbuilding of the body and prophetic 'words' should be expected when the whole body is functioning properly. What seemed to start for me as an individual gift has now very definitely become a gift for the church. Many others also receive and give 'words' which often prove to be very helpful.

Again and again we have found God is only too keen to speak and communicate with those who ask, seek and knock. As a church leader, I like to know someone has been right in small 'words' from God before I commit myself and our church to taking seriously more significant 'words' from that person. Often, however, we can only test 'words' by giving them. Mary often receives odd 'words'. On one occasion it was 'pink panther'. Pam, who was present and very much in need of prayer at the time, played in a subbuteo soccer league under the name of 'Pink Pamfers'. She was pleased to receive ministry.

Then there was 'Rupert Bear'. This time, a lady wearing a badge of Rupert Bear came forward and received long, deep and meaningful ministry from Mary herself.

When Mary gave the 'word' 'Hob Nail Boot' at another meeting, it was claimed by more than one person. A group had gone into a public house called the 'Hob Nail Boot' before the meeting and sensed God picking them out. But a lady needing considerable help and wanting prayer for her husband, also came forward because of his army connection where he wore hob nailed boots.

In each case, there was nothing physically wrong with the people concerned but the strange 'words' given led to very helpful and private ministry. None of the people would have asked for ministry on those occasions if God had not identified them and their private needs with non-revealing but very definite 'words'. When Mary has given ordinary 'words' she feels they have not always been as accurate or as helpful as her odd ones.

Once we have been right in small ways and learnt to identify the means by which God may communicate with us, then it may be right to take bigger risks – always, wherever possible, trying to be provably right or provably wrong – and always under the authority of godly leadership.

In the autumn of 1987 Bishop Colin Buchanan offered me a three months' sabbatical on behalf of the Birmingham Diocese as I had been vicar of Christ Church, Burney Lane since 1979. David Pytches suggested I wrote a book for Kingsway and they agreed. The final proofs were finished by April 1989 and in the summer of that year Kingsway asked me to consider writing a second book. This presented me with a major problem.

During my ten years as a vicar I had no clergy assistance of any kind in a parish of about 10,000 people. I was asked to do most of the weddings and funerals as well as run the church. In whose time could I write a second book? I had written much of the first one during my sabbatical. Could I write this one in the parish's time, the family time or my leisure time? I prayed about it as, humanly speaking, it did not seem right to say 'yes' to Kingsway.

As I asked God's opinion and waited in the silence, this thought came to me: 'When your first book comes out I will send you a retired Priest. He will enable you to write a second book, which I want you to do.' That was it. I began to map out the outline of 'Doing What Comes Supernaturally' and gave a verbal 'yes' to my publisher.

My first book, 'The Hot Line', came out in March 1990 and on Good Friday, returning from a week at Spring Harvest, I found a letter from Zimbabwe. It was from the sub-dean of Harare Cathedral, an Englishman by the name of Canon John Weller. He had just read my book; was sixty-five and very fit; owned a house in Birmingham; was thinking of retiring; would I like him to work free of charge in our parish for three years? I would. He and Jean have been a great blessing to us, the diocese and parish have had two clergymen for the price of one, and the book was published by Kingsway in 1992.

Sometimes, when we have learnt how our own receiver picks up messages from God, we can learn to trust his words for bigger issues.

**Summary**

Because the Spirit of God lives inside every believer it is often through our normal every day senses that God seeks to communicate with us.

We may:

* Smell his fragrance;

* Think his thoughts;

* See his pictures in our minds;

* Feel as he does – anger, sadness, joy, etc.;

* Register his pain touching our bodies;

* Hear his voice;

* Dream his dreams.

# 4

# Giving 'Words'

Whenever we think the God who speaks may have given us a message for someone else we face the nerve-wracking task of delivering it. In many church situations it may simply be a question of writing it out and giving it to the leader. I do not allow our church members to give prophetic messages of major guidance or judgement to individuals without showing them to me first. But somewhere along the line a 'word' which may be from God will have to be given before we can discover if it is likely to be a message from God. Once the idea of a lady at Whitley Bay with a bad leg due to polio had entered my head, I could not verify it without giving it.

The problem which has to be faced is that we may be right or we may be wrong.

In Matthew 16:16 Simon Peter said to Jesus, *'You are the Christ, the Son of the living God'*. Peter was right. Peter heard correctly a message from God. *'Jesus replied, "Blessed are you, Simon son of Jonah, for this was not revealed to you by man, but by my Father in heaven".'* (verse 17)

Five verses later *'Peter took him aside and began to rebuke him. "Never, Lord!" he said. "This shall never happen to you!" '* (verse 22).

This time Peter thought he was right, but was wrong. This thought did not come from God.

*'Jesus turned and said to Peter, "Get behind me, Satan! You*

*are a stumbling-block to me; you do not have in mind the things of God, but the things of men".'* (verse 23)

John the Baptist was *'filled with the Holy Spirit even from birth'* (Luke 1:15). Jesus said of him, *'among those born of women there is no-one greater than John'* (Luke 7:28). Yet he had doubts about Jesus. *'Are you the one who was to come'*, he asked, *'or should we expect someone else?'* (Luke 7:19).

We live in a world where wheat and weeds live side by side (Matthew 13:30). The voice of Satan came to Jesus, attacked and tried to deceive him (Matthew 4:1-10). Through his demonic slaves Satan will undoubtedly attack us as well. Some Christians have said to me, "When God speaks it will surely always be clear, obvious and accurate in every detail." Yes, if it is brought by an angel who shows himself clearly and audibly; yes, if God writes it on a wall for all to see; yes, if he thunders with a voice from the clouds that everyone hears.

But when the God who lives inside us by his Spirit communicates to us through our own senses, in my experience his normal way of speaking to Christians, we may not always receive aright. Sometimes a radio receiver crackles with interference; sometimes it is not tuned in properly. The problem is not with the transmitter or the person who is speaking but with the receiver. Who can claim to be a perfect receiver of God's message when he communicates from within us?

In Acts 11 Peter is asked to justify his action of taking the gospel to the Gentiles. In Acts, chapter 15 Peter, Barnabas and Paul give further accounts at the Council of Jerusalem on the same subject. The implication is that all are answerable to the church leaders and may at times be right or wrong. In Galatians 2:11 Paul writes, *'When Peter came to Antioch, I opposed him to his face, because he was clearly in the wrong.'* These people were in at the beginning of the Christian Church; filled with the Holy Spirit; healing the sick and raising the dead. Yet they knew in this present age they were not infallible.

26

Paul says, *'where there are prophecies, they will cease; where there are tongues, they will be stilled; where there is knowledge, it will pass away. For we know in part and we prophesy in part, but when perfection comes, the imperfect disappears.'* (1 Corinthians 13:8-10)

*'Two or three prophets should speak, and the others should weigh carefully what is said.'*          (1 Corinthians 14:29)

*'Do not put out the Spirit's fire; do not treat prophecies with contempt. Test everything. Hold on to the good.'*
(1 Thessalonians 5:19-21)

The New Testament is not as full as the Old Testament with phrases like *'thus says the Lord'*. The Holy Spirit has been poured out on all believers and the need to 'weigh', 'control' and 'test' messages from God has become very important. Consequently I believe it is vital that we develop appropriate language for giving 'words' that may be from God. Phrases such as:

'I believe God may be saying.'
'I offer this thought which might be from God.'
'Would I be right in thinking you…?'
'Forgive me if I'm wrong but I thought God might be nudging me into asking …'

This gives other Christians the opportunity to weigh, control and test what is being offered. The responsibility is passed from the individual to the body of Christ who can then prayerfully check out what is being said. If we humbly offer what we think God may have said to us, in love, then there should not be any need for wrong 'words' to be damaging or disastrous.

The Bible gives examples and teaching about giving 'words' from God to individuals (2 Samuel 12:7, John 1:47, 48, John 4:17, 18, Acts 5:9); to small groups (Matthew 26:21, Luke 22:19, 20, Mark 14:27, John 13:38); to churches (1 Corinthians 14); and to larger gatherings (Mark 5:30, Luke

8:45). Once we have begun to receive and recognise communications from God we can expect similar opportunities to come our way. We may also need to allow for mistakes at every level.

On one occasion I thought God was giving me a message for *an individual* concerning certain 'bondages' in her life. I never found out if I was right. I should have used the word 'problems'. The concept of 'bondages' had so many evil connotations in her mind that I was not allowed to give the rest of the communication. A *'word of wisdom'* is often needed to help us in giving a *'word of knowledge'* (1 Corinthians 12:8). I had wrongly assumed if the 'word' was from God it would automatically be well-received, no matter how I gave it.

On the other hand I gave two 'words' in a *small group* of five about bodily complaints, neither of which was claimed. I was completely wrong. But afterwards, as a result of taking a risk and failing, two individuals sought me out for ministry. Both found it helpful and one testified to it being an amazing event; she had never let anyone else minister to her before and God came in great power. The 'words' were wrong but the moment appeared to be right and God used it for his glory.

During a *church service* in Vancouver at which I was speaking I asked if there was a lady present called Doreen with a bad throat. No-one claimed it. Then someone said her friend had a relative called Doreen, she had a bad throat, and would that do? We prayed for her publicly with no apparent success. I realised afterwards I was wrong in doing this, not being prepared at the time to accept failure graciously.

At a *large gathering* of several thousand in Harrogate I heard John Wimber give a 'word' for George and Alice. Time went by and no-one claimed it. Eventually one of John's colleagues suggested it was meant for two friends called George and Alex. They were found later and everything else in the message fitted them. I was greatly encouraged to see how others more experienced than myself were not always 100% accurate.

It is my belief we do not have to be right all the time once we begin hearing from God but we do have to be loving. Providing we get some 'words' correct which build up the body of Christ and advance the kingdom of God, most people are not only willing to forgive mistakes but are often positively encouraged by others' failures to have a go themselves. Despite what they thought, they are not the only Christians in the world who are not yet perfect.

## Summary

Recognising that 'words' from God may be right, partly right or totally wrong should govern the way we learn to give them in various circumstances. Because we can be wrong when we give possible 'words' from God we:-

✳ Do not say, 'thus says the Lord';

✳ Are sensitive to the needs, feelings, and culture of the recipient;

✳ Do not embarrass others in public;

✳ Give 'words' in meetings without domination, manipulation or control, and wait for the Holy Spirit to convict people of the need to come forward;

✳ Pray for a *'word of wisdom'* to go with a *'word of knowledge'* when giving 'words' to individuals;

✳ Admit our mistakes graciously, learn from them, and try again.

# 5

# Claiming 'Words'

When I gave the 'word' in Whitley Bay about a lady with a bad leg due to polio, she rose to her feet and claimed it. Sometimes, however, especially in Britain, people are reluctant to claim 'words' publicly even when detailed and accurate.

There are those who believe if it is God who is speaking, a 'word' will always be claimed and always be correct in every detail. I can understand this desire for certainty. Looking like an idiot at the front of a meeting is not something I particularly enjoy. But in my experience spiritual gifts do not cut across other Biblical principles. God has given limited freedom and responsibility to mankind and he does not withdraw it every time he speaks. Only a few people received the words of Jesus when he was on earth and he allowed many to reject him. On the day of Pentecost some received God's words given through the disciples: *'some, however, made fun of them and said, "They have had too much wine" '* (Acts 2:13). In the parable of the sower Jesus indicates God's words will only be received and bear fruit in some people (Matthew 13:3-23).

In Luke 8:43-48 Jesus feels power go out of him and publicly asks *'who touched me?'* (Luke 8:45). Initially there is no response but Jesus remains calm and firm, *'Someone touched me'* (Luke 8:46). Eventually the embarrassed lady owns up and receives further affirmation and blessing. It seems to me we can help people to claim God's 'words' by remaining calm and firm and if necessary waiting for the Holy Spirit to come and convict.

But even if a 'word' which is given to us is accurate it is our responsibility to decide whether to receive and act upon the message which accompanies it. Because 'words' can be right, partly right or wrong it is up to those who are listening to decide what to do with what is given.

In Acts 21:10-14 Agabus informs Paul that the Holy Spirit says he will be bound in Jerusalem and handed over to the Gentiles. The Christians of Caesarea, which included in their number Philip, his four prophetic daughters, and Dr. Luke pleaded with Paul not to go to Jerusalem. But Paul went, believing it was God's will for him to be arrested. Paul believed God's word and acted upon it as he saw fit.

King Ahab asked the prophet Micaiah about going to war against Ramoth Gilead (1 Kings 22:15-40). Micaiah replies *'attack and be victorious'* (verse 15). The king recognises this is not from God and asks for the truth. The prophet informs him he will attack and be killed. Ahab puts Micaiah in prison, attacks Ramoth Gilead, and is killed.

Ahab seemed to know the truth and yet he could not bring himself to act accordingly. It is the responsibility of the hearer to receive or reject a 'word' from God.

At a joint meeting of local churches I had what felt like a bad time. I believed God had given me four 'words' which I mentioned publicly. Three were not claimed and I think they were probably totally wrong. The fourth one went something like this.

"I think there may be a man here who has a lump on his head. No-one in the church knows about it because it is always covered over by his hair. I believe God wants to heal him and remove it."

Immediately Bill claimed it. He showed us the considerable lump which no-one, including myself, knew existed. People gathered round, one or two laid on hands and asked God to come on Bill who felt greatly blessed. But nothing physical happened. The service continued and I felt something of a failure.

32

Afterwards Carole was convicted to speak to Bill. "If God has said it," she said, "and the 'word' does seem to fit exactly, I think we should believe him. I will pray for you regularly to be healed," and her friend Anj also prayed.

Bill agreed with Carole; they both continued to pray for healing and encouraged one another each week in church. I ignored them and let them get on with it. I was too despondent about the other 'words' and did not feel full of faith.

The large lump on Bill's head had been there for thirty years before I gave the 'word'. After three months it seemed to be getting smaller. After a year it had gone completely. It was a tremendous encouragement to Bill and Carole and to me. It is our responsibility to act upon 'words' which God gives us with determination.

Because 'words' which appear to be from God may be wrong I believe it is important we do not feel pressurised to receive a 'word' which someone else says is from God without questioning it. Ananias (Acts 9:13) and Peter (Acts 10:14) questioned 'words' which they thought were from God and God confirmed them without reproach.

On one occasion I believed God gave me a message for a vicar called John. A clergyman named John wondered if it might be for him so I gave the rest of the message about someone who was discouraged, just as it had come to me. "No," said John and his wife, "that doesn't fit at all."

They were absolutely right. It would have been very easy to try and be nice to me and make some of it fit. Maybe this part – occasionally I do feel a bit down – and so on. But it wasn't for them and they recognised it. It can be very dangerous to try and fit a 'word' when it doesn't fit us. We may subconsciously start becoming what we are not – what God does not want us to be.

On the other hand there can be 'words' given which in detail are not completely accurate which we rightly receive because God anoints us. It can be like a sermon when one part, one sentence or phrase suddenly hits us – we know it is God speaking directly to us and we may not hear any more of the sermon.

I remember for example, giving a 'word' for a young, fair-haired girl which a middle-aged silver-haired lady claimed. Years later she still describes the moment as a life-changing one when she felt God was speaking directly to her. Needless to say she had once been a young, fair-haired girl and the rest of the message spoke into her current situation.

Sometimes a 'word' is given which fits a person who knows on that occasion it is not for them. I gave one 'word' in a very small group for a lady with a damaged left arm. One lady present had years before burnt her left arm which was still scarred but as she prayed she sensed it was not for her. She regularly received very accurate communications from God and this was shown to be the case again when another lady claimed the 'word' and was greatly helped by prayer.

Some 'words' from God are so specific they are meant for only one person but some are less detailed and are intended for more than one. On the night before he died Jesus said, *'one of you will betray me'* (Mark 14:18), Peter *'will disown me three times'* (Mark 14:30), but to everyone present he said, *'you will all fall away'* (Mark 14:27).

Occasionally when I give a 'word' publicly nobody claims it, until afterwards. Then a person will often say, 'did anyone claim the one about…' implying that if no-one else did they will. Recently a friend gave me six 'words' which I gave to a meeting and one and a half were claimed publicly. During the course of the following week every 'word' was eventually owned by someone, and one 'word' was claimed by eight different people even though no-one had come forward for it on the night.

It does not matter if someone else claims a 'word' from God

which I think also fits me. I always encourage everyone to receive ministry if they think a 'word' may be for them, no matter how many others have claimed it first. God is quite capable of putting his finger on several different people at once, touching them with his love, and encouraging them to take more steps in following him.

Frequently we British Christians are very passive in our meetings. We sit like sponges soaking up all that comes our way fully expecting someone else to minister to us. But when a leader sticks his neck out and is prepared to take a risk he deserves our love, support, encouragement and prayer. As we pray for the leader he is more likely to receive a clearer message; as we encourage him it may help him to take a risk again; as we respond and claim the 'words' so we minister to him and the whole body of Christ. "Yes, we do want God to speak to us in our services."

On one occasion I attended a mid-week session at St. Thomas' Church in Sheffield. I sat on the very back row on the right-hand side with four others. After worship and a talk one of the leaders invited the Holy Spirit to come and minister to us. Power came upon me and I sat down. In my mind I saw myself with coils of chains locked all around me. I asked the Lord what it was and soon began to realise it was to do with my father and our relationship. He had been dead a few years but I knew I still had work to do. I repented of sins I had committed, forgave father for his and released him into Jesus' hands. Feeling quite emotional I saw all the chains in my mind fall away and myself stepping clear of them. The love and forgiveness of God then began to wash over me.

Suddenly I heard a voice on the microphone. "I believe the Lord is showing me there is a minister sitting on the back row, right-hand side. I can see chains wrapped all around him. If he comes forward we will pray for his release."

Nothing could be more specific. There were only five of us in that pew. I was quite sure none of the others were ministers. And what about the chains? Ah, but... he was wrong wasn't he? I'd already been released and they had gone. I failed to go forward and stayed in my seat.

I felt guilty all the way back to Birmingham. I could have ministered to him by owning up. Maybe he'd never know. I wrote when I arrived home and apologised. I have always been very grateful ever since whenever people have responded to 'words' I have given which I believed were from God. Because *we know in part and prophesy in part'* (1 Corinthians 13:9), and *'see but a poor reflection as in a mirror'* (1 Corinthians 13:12), it is important that we encourage one another by actively responding and claiming 'words' which may be from God.

## Summary

\* It is our responsibility to claim 'words' from God which seem to fit us.

\* If the Spirit of God convicts us it may be right to claim a 'word' which is only partly accurate.

\* Responding positively to 'words' given as from God which are appropriate will encourage the body of Christ to seek God's face, step out in faith, obey his commands and advance his kingdom.

# 6

# Confirming a 'Word'

When I gave the 'word' at Whitley Bay about the lady with a weak leg she stood up and claimed it. At that point we could say the information I believed to be from God was found to be accurate.

Micaiah the prophet said King Ahab would die in battle. As they took him away to prison he declared, *'If you ever return safely, the Lord has not spoken through me'* (Kings 22:28).

I believe it is right to expect 'words' from God which contain information to be correct. This does not mean any 'word' given which is accurate is necessarily from God, but it does mean any 'word' given which is totally inaccurate is not from God. Trial and error is a good starting place. It removes obviously wrong 'words' and this is why I think anyone learning to hear the voice of God should be willing to risk 'words' which may be provably wrong. *'If what a prophet proclaims in the name of the Lord does not take place or come true, that is a message the Lord has not spoken'* (Deuteronomy 18:22).

Unfortunately there can be 'words' given which are accurate and still not from God. In Philippi Paul and Silas *'were met by a slave girl who had a spirit by which she predicted the future'* (Acts 16:16). When Paul cast the Spirit out of her in the name of Jesus Christ *'the owners of the slave girl realised that their hope of making money was gone'* (Acts 16:19). This incident led to Paul and Silas being imprisoned. It would seem from all the fuss which was made that the slave girl really did predict the future but was unable to do it once the evil spirit had been cast out.

Paul writes to the Thessalonians,

> *'The coming of the lawless one will be in accordance with the work of Satan displayed in all kinds of counterfeit miracles, signs and wonders'* (2 Thessalonians 2:9)

With the rise of interest in the occult in this country belief in correct 'words' from wrong sources is no longer confined to Voodoo practitioners or witch doctors abroad. Some will now be familiar with the practice of mediums giving accurate 'words of knowledge' in spiritualist meetings.

In many instances the yardstick of Scripture will help us to test what is from God. Is the 'word' in keeping with the principles of the Bible and does the fruit which it produces advance the kingdom of God? Mediums often claim the word is from a deceased relative; a practice which is forbidden in the Bible (Leviticus 19:31). We therefore declare their 'words' to be not from God however accurate they may appear.

In some ways prophets are easier to test than prophecies – by their fruits you will recognise them (Matthew 17:20) – but it is not always an accurate test for the 'words' they give. Godly mature Christians can be wrong and new immature Christians can sometimes be more open to receive unmerited freely given spiritual gifts.

If a 'word' passes the accuracy test and does not contradict the principles of Scripture then I believe it needs to be further approved by the Spirit-filled body of Christ and its leaders. In Acts, chapter 15 Peter, Paul and Barnabas allow the apostles and elders of the Jerusalem church to test their guidance for taking the gospel to the Gentiles. In the end James concluded: *'It seemed good to the Holy Spirit and to us...'* (Acts 15:28). Paul teaches, *'Two or three prophets should speak, and others should weigh carefully what is said'* (1 Corinthians 14:29).

After the lady in Whitley Bay stood up I gave the rest of the message. I believed God not only wanted to encourage her to lay hands on the sick but to realise her own disability had already equipped her with sensitivity for the task. The body of Christ confirmed the 'word'. Those who knew her well nodded or hummed approval. Most people who are unwell like to receive ministry from those who know how it feels to be ill. This was just the person they wanted to lay hands on them when they were sick. The 'word' seemed good to the assembly and to the Holy Spirit within them.

With many 'words' like this the ultimate confirmation is to see if they advance the kingdom of God and produce the fruit of the Spirit. When someone's lifestyle is changed and becomes more like Jesus as a result of responding positively to a 'word', then we can be reasonably sure it is from the Lord. Time will tell whether the lady at Whitley Bay receives the gift of faith and people are healed as well as comforted by her ministry in the name of Jesus.

*Words of knowledge* are in many ways easier to test than prophecies because they often contain verifiable information and may provide immediate fruit. At a weekend in Shropshire as the Holy Spirit was moving amongst us the words, 'crippling arthritis' flashed into my mind. One person claimed it and after prayer in the name of Jesus could open her mouth freely without pain. Prior to the weekend she had not been able to attend the dentist's because of pain and immobility in the jaw. Those of us who were present felt reasonably sure it was God who was speaking.

**Summary for testing 'Words of Knowledge'**

✳ We test for accuracy of information imparted.

✳ We check the 'word' against the principles of the Bible.

✳ We allow the body of Christ under godly authority to confirm the 'word'.

✳ We see if the 'word' given and claimed advances the kingdom of God.

Prophecies are different. They normally contain messages which are not so easy to verify on the spot and yet church leaders like myself often have to make instant decisions about whether or not to give them. I am regularly given bits of paper at church, or letters arrive containing possible prophecies. I have a drawer full of them in my study. This is how I tend to react to them.

1) There are those which are given as personal encouragements to me. Azariah approached Asa, King of Judah with this 'word'. *'The Lord is with you when you are with him. If you seek him, he will be found by you'* (2 Chronicles 14:2). There was a bit more but nothing particularly specific, nevertheless it inspired Asa to tackle major reforms.

Many 'words' which are given to me are like this one. Sometimes they quote Scripture. I read them, pray and thank God for them, file them in my drawer marked prophecies, and carry on with my daily tasks. From time to time God reminds me of a prophecy and then I take it out for further consideration. I do not quickly throw away those I believe may be from God.

Often the most helpful ones arrive when I am feeling low or tired. Sometimes they come when it has seemed the whole world was against me. Zechariah warns us not to despise *'the day of small things'* (Zechariah 4:10), and I am always grateful for encouraging 'words' however insignificant they may appear to others.

Nevertheless such communications even if encouraging still need to be tested against Scripture. Are they encouraging me to do God's work as Azariah encouraged Asa, or are they encouraging me to sin? This is why good Bible knowledge is important in testing 'words'.

When people quote Scripture, as specifically for me from God

I always examine the context very carefully. Somebody once gave me a passage from the book of Job suggesting it was God's word to me for the moment. "That is strange," I replied, "it is one of Job's comforters speaking whom God later said was not right."

There is an occult practice called 'bibliomancy' in which people dip into a Bible at random for guidance. If we use the Scriptures like a pack of tarot cards we should not be surprised if it is not God's word we hear. In the wilderness Satan tried to tempt Jesus by quoting the Bible out of context. This can be very misleading. It says in the Bible, for example, *'There is no God'* (Psalm 14:1). The full context, however, changes the meaning. *'The fool has said in his heart, "There is no God." '* The context is important. Relevant Bible passages, applied according to context, can focus God's truth on a certain problem but this is why good Bible knowledge is important in testing 'words'.

As a general rule I find in practice that 'words' of individual encouragement can normally be received gladly by those well versed in the Scriptures, without any great need to spend a lot of time on testing.

2. Sometimes, however, people give me 'messages from God' which are not encouraging. Whenever these come I always look very carefully at the content for proposed solutions. Discernment without love is criticism. Satan is the accuser of the brethren (Revelations 12:10). It is not very clever or helpful simply to point out other people's weaknesses or where the church is going wrong. The gospel of Jesus Christ is good news. A word from God will not only pinpoint the problem but outline the way forward.

If it is personal criticism of me, then I always show it to my wife Carol or my closest friends. Often they say, "This is his own personal hang-up or problem", and advise me to ignore it. Occasionally those nearest to me encourage me to take note. Following one 'word' I asked a friend: "Do you think I am a forceful dominating personality?" "Let us put it this way," he replied. "I cannot remember too many situations where you have not got your own way." The message came home and stuck. I'm still working on it.

I do not easily pass on 'words' of criticism and judgement for our church unless it also contains hope. Jonah told Nineveh they were about to perish. They all repented. God forgave them. This is the character of God. We do need to be challenged about our failures, shortcomings and sins but so that the kingdom of God may be advanced; so that we may become more like Jesus; so that he may be glorified in our midst. 'Words' which may be critical but offer that hope may be worth sharing. I normally test them in our prayer group first before launching them on the entire congregation.

The Holy Spirit sometimes comes to convict of sin (John 15:8). After I have read a possible challenging prophecy to our prayer meeting I will then ask the Holy Spirit to come and do what he wants to do. If several of us are then convicted of sin or failure in regard to the words of the prophecy I may then feel it is appropriate to share it with the whole church. "I think Fred needs to hear this" does not count, in my opinion. "I, myself, feel convicted by this 'word'," is the reaction which confirms it to me, if said by several people. If the prophecy also contains reasonable and biblical suggestions about how we might seek to rectify the problem I will normally then give it to the full assembly. Only time will tell if it really was God speaking as we see if it is fulfilled.

3) Occasionally 'words' come which are not only specific but suggest immediate action. These cannot be filed in a drawer but require testing as soon as possible.

Recently I was due to speak at a weekend in Shropshire. Eight days before it started I received a prophecy in the post saying the Lord wanted me to break bread every day between then and the weekend. There was also mention of the blood of Christ so I took it to mean celebrating Holy Communion every day.

42

This presented me with an immediate problem. As an Anglican vicar I am only allowed to preside at a Eucharist and celebrate Holy Communion with others present. I considered the following points:-

a) The person who sent the prophecy had been provably right several time before.

b) Celebrating Holy Communion every day for eight days was a good thing to do and not an impossible task. The activity itself was commanded by our Lord Jesus Christ as recorded in the gospels.

c) I was extremely busy and under a lot of pressure at the time.

As I could not obey this prophecy alone I took it to the house Bible-study where I was going that evening, for testing. I read it, shared the above three points, and then we asked the Holy Spirit to speak to us. Several people shared positive thoughts and Mary received the words 'nine o'clock in the morning'. This was interesting. We take our children to school just before nine o'clock. The only time after that when I could celebrate Holy Communion every day until the Shropshire weekend without altering my diary was nine o'clock in the morning. On some days every moment was already booked from 9.30a.m. onwards. The people present committed themselves to coming whenever they could.

We obeyed the prophecy. Numbers at the Holy Communion were never less than six. The weekend seemed to go particularly well; all the 'words' we gave were claimed; some healing and deliverance took place and many felt the power of God in special ways, a few for the first time. The final session was particularly moving when a wave of God's compassion for the lost swept over the gathering and several people began to weep unashamedly. I am sure God was anointing them with the gift of evangelism.

Many of us found the daily Communion services so helpful that in Holy Week, two weeks later, we did it again. Once more attendance was never less than six and sometimes considerably more. All who came seemed to find them helpful.

Those who were involved with this prophecy now feel it was a 'word from the Lord'. This was how we tested it.

## Summary of tests used on our Prophecy

* The person giving it was known to us. Her 'words' had been right before.

* The activity suggested was very much in keeping with Scripture.

* A further 'word' from a known person solved our practical problems.

* The Body of Christ approved of it.

* The Body of Christ committed themselves to it.

* There appeared to be fruit of the Spirit coming from our obedience.

## Conclusion

The God who speaks lives inside every born-again Christian. Because of this we are not only the temple of the Holy Spirit but potentially receivers of divine communications. Once we begin to expect God to speak to us from within ourselves and through our own senses we shall begin to hear him. Acting upon his 'words', giving them to others with love and sensitivity, claiming them when appropriate and allowing the body of Christ to test them all will often empower and equip us to advance God's kingdom more fruitfully. Abraham, Moses, Elijah, Peter and Paul would not have done great things for God without hearing from him first.

Is there a word from the Lord? Ask him and see.